THE SILENT STRUGGLES
of a Saved Woman

The Silent Struggles of a Saved Woman
Copyright © 2023 by Barbara Delores Thomas

Published in the United States of America
ISBN   Paperback: 979-8-89091-205-3
ISBN   eBook: 979-8-89091-206-0

All rights reserved. No part of this publication may be reproduced, stored in a retrieval system or transmitted in any way by any means, electronic, mechanical, photocopy, recording or otherwise without the prior permission of the author except as provided by USA copyright law.

The opinions expressed by the author are not necessarily those of ReadersMagnet, LLC.

ReadersMagnet, LLC
10620 Treena Street, Suite 230 | San Diego, California, 92131 USA
1.619. 354. 2643 | www.readersmagnet.com

Book design copyright © 2023 by ReadersMagnet, LLC. All rights reserved.

Cover design by Tifanny Curaza
Interior design by Daniel Lopez

THE SILENT STRUGGLES
of a Saved Woman

BARBARA DELORES THOMAS

ReadersMagnet, LLC

Table of Contents

From the Pit to the Stage 1
I Suffered in Silence 5
Joy Does Come In The Morning 6
I Had To Change My Perspective 7
God Answers Prayers 8
The Blessing of Endurance 10
Suffering for A Purpose 11
God Keeps His Promises 12
We cannot hide who we are. Our character will give us away! 15
Two Wrongs Do Not Make a Right 17
I Struggled In Silence For Years 19
Money Cannot Buy Happiness 20
Where Do I Go From Here? 22
My God Is an On-time God, Yes, He Is 25
A Dream Came True 26
I Went From The Pit To The Stage!!! 27
No Weapons Formed Against Me Shall Prosper 30
Trusting God In A Crises 33
Holding On To The Words God Gave Me 35
Forgiveness Releases A Harvest Of Blessings 37
God Will Restore What The Enemy Has Stolen 39

From the Pit to the Stage

I was saved at the age of ten in the Kittrell First Baptist Church where I grew up. For the most part, I encountered a good life. My mom and dad took really good care of us. Now that I look back on my life, it was normal for the most part.

My father was a brick mason and my mom work in various jobs to help make ends meet. We enjoyed being with my mom's family, only because we didn't know Dad's family very well.

The people that we did know were wonderful to us and they made sure Dad took care of us. We were fortunate growing up to have such great people in our family on both sides. My father was the only child because his mom died a few weeks after he was born. His grandmother raised him after his mother passed away. Her children saw him as their brother, but in reality, he was their nephew.

One aunt was a kind and generous woman, her name was Aunt Sarah. She lived in New Jersey all of her life. She would send money to help support her mom and nephew. One day, Aunt Sarah hit the lottery and she wanted to build her mom a house. The house was small because she did not come down to watch over her investment. She was very disappointed in the size of the house due to the fact she trusted the contractor to build it to her specifications. By the time she came to see it, there was nothing she could do. Even though it was small it was big enough for their parents and three children to grow up in.

When I was very young, my Aunt Sarah died. Her husband was left with her estate because they had no children of their own. He was so kind to us, especially my mom. He treated us like we were his blood family. One day he calls me over to where he was sitting. I sat on his lap and he asked me this question. He wanted to know if I wanted to go to college and if I thought my sibling wanted to as well. My answer was yes, we do. I really was not sure about my brother and sister. I just knew I wanted to.

I never thought a lot about it again until he died. He left me and my sibling all of his estate, including his car. We were all so young, so my dad was appointed executive administrator over our money and 80 shares of Sears, Roebuck, and Co. stock. My uncle was a smart man, so no one could get any money for any purpose unless I called or wrote a letter to the lawyer. It is amazing to think about the responsibility that I had as a child.

Daddy wanted to add a bathroom and a living room to the house, so I had to write a letter and tell the lawyer what we wanted to do with our money. As time went on, I graduated from high school and I decided to go to community college in my hometown of Kittrell, North Carolina. I was always afraid to do things even in high school, so I kept to myself and kept my head in my books. I had very low self-esteem and I was very insecure and introverted. So, attending college at home was fine with me. All I had to do was go to school because everything was paid for by my Uncle Sim, Aunt Sarah's husband. So, in September 1968, I started at Kittrell Junior College. I was so excited but fearful at the same time. One day, as I got out of my girlfriend's car, I passed a young man sitting on the dorm steps. He made a pass at me. I responded in a way that left him thinking. First, he called me bb. So, I wanted to know how he knew my name. Then I said, "If you think you are going to get anything from me, you have the wrong person." Later, he told me that the Lord told him that I will be his wife. He signed my college class book and mentions it, which I still have today.

I struggled with staying saved and staying a virgin until marriage. Not because I was hot to have sex. There were a few guys who were always hitting on me. Don't get me wrong, I like the attention but I was not ready for sex, and I did not want to hurt my family.

I always said I did not want to hurt my mom and dad or God. When my husband came along, it became harder because he was so nice. Even my dad liked him and let him drive his car (which was not normal for him to do). I was really afraid that I would lose him, and I did not want him to think I was weird. So sometimes we would play around but never was there any intercourse.

So, in June 1969, my husband, and I were married. I was so afraid that night that my marriage was not consummated until we got to New Jersey to live for the summer (June).

While we were there, my husband had a job working on the boardwalk, and I got my first job in the laundry.

One day, it rains so hard that parts of the city flooded, even where I worked. The rains flooded in the building and the water came up pass my knees. I panic because I had never seen anything like that. My husband came and rescued me, and we walked home together.

We enjoyed being in the city together but we wanted to live in Henderson, North Carolina so we decided to move to Kittrell. God bless us and the pastor who married us (who was a friend of our family) knew we were looking for a place to live in Henderson. He heard of woman who had a beautiful home in Henderson for rent. She called us and she came down from New York to meet us. After meeting us, she decided to let us live in her beautiful two-story house for free. All we had to do was take care of it. Everything we needed was in the house. It was fully furnished and all we had to do was to bring in our clothes. We were happy just the two of us, but it was all about to change.

I Suffered in Silence

We had our first big fight over a set of tires that he brought for his dad. He lied and said he didn't make the purchase. That started me to wonder if I had made a mistake. I felt like his family meant more to him than me. We didn't have any extra money for tires for someone else's car!!! My parents were helping us, and he was giving the money away that we needed. My trust in him was broken because of his lie. From that point and after that we began to have conflict. One day, we got into an argument, and he came at me, so I grab a pair of scissors to protect myself. I lunged at him and hit him in his elbow with the scissors. I could not believe this was happening to me. The marriage I had waited for was now turning to violence. Even my dad came over to talk with us, but things were starting to crumble. Then he started to lie about little things on his job, and my trust in him was taking a toll on me.

Joy Does Come In The Morning

With fear still governing my heart, I told my husband it was time for me to have his child.

We agreed and we conceived that night, and nine months later our son was born. It was a joyous time for us and things seem to get better. We lived in Henderson and went to church in Oxford, North Carolina. God had blessed us with a beautiful home rent-free. The house had four bedrooms, two full baths, a large kitchen, a den, a living room with solid wood floors, and a large back porch. I was so blessed and happy because I was only 15 minutes away from my family.

I Had To Change My Perspective

One day, I didn't attend church service and my husband came home to announce that he was called to the ministry. I was happy because I always wanted to marry a preacher. They were all good men, I thought, and this was based on the Baptist preachers I knew. Life was good until he received word from a pastor that he was supposed to move home. He was told that the Lord spoke and that he was supposed to help his father in ministry. I was devastated because I had never heard anything like a message from God to a person (remember I am Baptist). So of course, I am upset with the idea of moving. We had made plans to build or buy a house in Kittrell near my family, and I was excited. Now this sudden change caught me by surprise. Soon my fears, insecurity, and co-dependency surfaced. I would have to leave all that I knew and love to follow a man and his life.

God Answers Prayers

Following God when I didn't know what to do, I put my fate into God's hands. I told him that if I needed to go with my husband, to let me have my own furniture to take with me. Remember we live in a house that belongs to someone else, everything belongs to her except our clothes.

God really knows how to get you where you need to be, even if you don't want to. I turned to God, the only one I could trust for answers. My pastor had preached on praying to God for directions and answers. So I prayed and went on a fast.

I lived in the same town as my mother's Aunt Hattie. She had a beautiful home with very nice furniture. She became very ill and she died of cancer. Her sisters came down from New York to look after her estate. Since they lived in New York, they did not want to take any furniture with them. Yes, you know what happens next. They gave me most of her furniture, and other things to set up the house. What could I say to God? He gave me what I ask for in the prayer, so we moved to Southern Pines, North Carolina. My husband rented an apartment which I did not like. After we put our things in the house, I felt better. Later, we noticed that the place was infected with fleas. My husband and my son were bitten from head to toe. We could no longer stay there even after it was sprayed.

We moved across town, and my husband and I found work at the same factory. Then with little notice, we were both laid off. We had brought our first new car, not used, and we were in a new apartment, but now with no job. With just a little unemployment, things became tense sometimes, and even again physical. Things could not get any worse, or I thought, I now had to deal with his family. I had never been treated with such disrespect in my life by some of the family. Again, the fear almost brought me to tears. It is like I could do nothing right. The more I tried to please them, the worse I felt. I could not run back home. I just needed to face my fear and stay there. God began to bless us regardless of the problems.

The Blessing of Endurance

In 1974, my husband was called to pastor in Mt. Gilead, North Carolina. His father placed us there to start a ministry. It was an old house that had no bathroom, and no running water or heater. We both were faithful to that church for 13 years. We drove over an hour with our children to get to the service. Even though it was hard at first, I learned to love the people, because they became my family. The McKinney's took care of us as well as they could. One day, Sister Annie and her children made sure we had food after we were laid off from our jobs in Southern Pines. Sister Annie's sister, Kay, always invited us to her home when we had to stay over for another service. Many times, I cooked or warmed our food on a little hot plate which I still have along with the serving pans that I carried our food in. One day, my husband announced that it was time to leave Mt. Gilead and go start a ministry in Albemarle, North Carolina. It was only about 40 minutes away because now we can have a place with running water and a bathroom. Praise God!!! Sister Annie and her children moved to Albemarle too. It is amazing that ever since 1974, I am still part of their family, and they are part of my family. They are great, faithful, and loyal people to me.

Suffering for A Purpose

We started out in the Albemarle Hotel. Then as people began to come, we moved to our own building. Later we brought the whole building. Things were getting better between us and we started to work in ministry together. I was told by his father not to go to work.

My job was to stay home and pray up the church. I went to prayer, kept my house, and served my husband. I experienced the hand of God many, many times. He always answered even the smallest of prayers and my husband knew that I had the gift of intercession.

Whenever there was a need, I would pray. This was nothing new for me, because as a child prayer was part of my life. One day, my husband ask me to pray with him about leaving his job. He wanted to stop driving back and forth to Southern Pines to work. We were renting the house we lived in. We wanted to buy it, so again I prayed to the lord. If God blessed us to buy the house, my husband would work full-time for God. You guessed it, God blessed us to buy it. My husband on the other hand was fearful and I said, "You told God you would leave the job. God answered our prayer, so you must leave the job by faith." He did, but I had to overcome any fear I had, by faith too.

God Keeps His Promises

Years went by and God began to bless us, just like he said he would do. One day after prayer, a woman by the name of Sister Teresa Thomas came into our lives. She was like an angel sent by God to bless us. She was not a relative of my husband, but she became one of my spiritual daughters. She provided everything that we needed to make our lives better. One day she asked to see the cabinets in my kitchen. She prayed that they would never go bare. Then she said, "God just spoke to me while I was praying. God told me to buy your groceries for a year but to stop the supply after the year." Sister Teresa did exactly what the Lord instructed her to do for us. Then she helped us with other things like buying Christmas gifts and even school clothes for my children and much more.

The church grew and we needed to build. A word from the Lord came about us finding a property to build. I believed that word so much that I started to look for the land. Finally, one day, I called a realtor about a house I saw. I wanted to open a house for displaced women. As it turns out the place was not a house, but an apartment.

I had come to realize that there are no accidents with God. Later that same day, the realtor call back to speak to me about some land. Little did I know that it would turn out to be the land that I had been looking for.

My husband did not seem excited, so two other ladies went with me to see the land. Not only did I know it was the land, but we claim all 34 acres of it as ours. That evening, my husband went to see it. He was in shock, but he approved of it too.

We told the church about the land and began to make plans to buy it. My husband asks everyone to sacrifice and not buy Christmas gifts but give the money to buy the land. We all agreed, and we paid for all thirty-four acres (about half the area of a large shopping mall). It was a happy time for all of us. God had blessed the people with their own businesses and many of them were living in upscaled homes in beautiful neighborhoods. People were moving from other cities to be close to the ministry, and wonderful things were happening. To make a long story short, we built the building. It would accommodate six hundred people, and it was 10,000 square feet (about twice the area of a basketball court). It made the front page of our newspaper and even the city was excited for us.

Little did I know that years later my life would change forever. The beautiful life that I believe I had started to change.

The more material things we acquired, the more distant we seem to grow. Ministry was all he seemed to really care about, and all we talked about. We began to have frequent arguments over trivial things, his character, and how he treated me and others too. It seemed like he really could not let things go even after the apologies. We smiled in the public eye, but privately things were changing. Being the person that I was, I tried to fix things. I started out buying books and tapes on marriage. I would share what I was learning. He was interested at times, but other times he would make fun of the books. I sent in prayers request, and placed Bible quotes over my bathroom door, declaring a good marriage. Nothing seemed to work, so one day his mother told us we needed to get professional counseling. I look up a Christian counselor in Charlotte. He just happened to be a former pastor. He charged us one hundred dollars an hour and I felt that it would be worth every dollar if he could help us. We started off well, and he gave us books and assignments to do together. As time went on, my husband would get upset and stop reading the books and we found ourselves back to where we were again. One day we went to the counselor, and he wanted to know how things were going. He had told us to bring any problems to the session and we would talk about them. I knew that my husband would never mention a problem, because he had spent most of the time pretending that everything was fine at home. So, I mention a situation that was happening with the members of the church. The people came to me about certain things and conflicts that they were having with him. I listened to them, but my advice was they needed to talk with him. I was not in the wrong for listening, but he believes that I should have never let them tell me anything about him. When I bought this up in session, he was okay, but when we left the session, he told me that I just wanted to make him look bad. So, from then on, I never bought anything else up in the sessions. We paid $100.00 an hour for 8 months but we never resolved anything.

We cannot hide who we are. Our character will give us away!

Your Gift Will Get You Inside a Door, But Your Character Will Keep You There

One day, the counselor asks him a question, and for the first time, the counselor saw a side of him that shocked him. He jumped up out of the chair and said, "I am finished with this. I won't be back." He left the room and he drove off. I really thought that he had left me in Charlotte which terrified me. After the session was over, he came back only to pick me up outside, and never again did he attend the session. He took me several more times, but he would not go in again. So, he tells everyone that we went to counseling, but it did not help our marriage. I felt like things could not get any worse, but I was so wrong. For years, he threatened to leave me whenever he was mad at me. Yet, he always came back and said he was just joking. I lived in a state of confusion, fear, and anxiety all my married life. I came into the marriage with a co-dependent behavior. I had never been with any man other than my husband, so I depended on him for all outside acceptance and validation. When I looked back now, my husband became my god, and I believed that I could never live without him.

Two Wrongs Do Not Make a Right

Over time I realized that I was also changing and not in a positive way. I allowed the situations in my life to get me out of character. I fought to survive by doing some of the things he was doing to hurt me. For instance, when I wanted him to talk to me and work out whatever problem we were having, I would do things that forced him to stay and talk. Sometimes I would hide his car keys so he could not leave the house or hide his wallet. I just wanted to talk and not fight with him, but it only made him more upset with me. I would try to block him from leaving by standing in his way, and pleading for us to talk and for him not to leave me. I love him more than my own life, but I did not know how to fix it. My prayers were hitting the walls and they were not being answered by God or as I thought. One day I just wanted to spend some time with him, no shopping at the mall and no fancy restaurant. Just quality time talking. But it turned violent. We were talking and it ended in another argument. I was afraid and he was so angry that I felt he would do something to hurt me. I ran out of the room and went to my bedroom, and pulled a weapon at him.

He was afraid of weapons, so he ran into the bathroom. I do not think he ever forgave me for that. He tells people about the incident, but he never tells people why I did it. I forgave him when he pulled the chair from under me, and I fell on the floor. I forgave him, but sometimes a person can see another person's wrong but not their own. There is a story in the Bible that mention how David judged another man's actions but when the prophet came to him, he did not realize that Nathan the Prophet was talking about David's own sins.

I prayed for peace and deliverance because I just wanted to be happy. My husband took care of me financially, and he made sure everyone knew it. I got everything I wanted, except for my emotional and psychological needs, which were bankrupt. I had to smile through many days when all I wanted to do was cry. I would pray on my way to church to smile, so that no one could tell by my face. One day, I overheard one of the men say, "What is wrong with her? She is not smiling. She must have done something to Pastor." That is just how people will judge you without knowing all the details. They see what is happening, but they never ask why it is happening. I had to suppress my feelings to keep the peace around the church people because I did not want to expose him or my pain, so I hid it from everyone as much as I could. I did not have friends because I was the pastor's wife. I was told you do not do fellowship with them unless it was at church.

I Struggled In Silence For Years

My family loved my husband so much and they were so proud of us, so I never mentioned my troubles to them. I always wanted his father to marry us on our 25th wedding anniversary, which he did. Our church gave us a beautiful celebration. My family came and so did Mrs. Yates who allowed us to stay in her vacation home in Henderson rent-free. It was beautiful and he showed such love for me again. It was so joyful living in my wonderland life. Years would go by before everything that was in the dark came to light. The reason that people did not believe what I was going through is that I struggled in silence. I have learned that in many cases of abuse, the victims are silent and when everything comes out, the victims are made to look like it is all their fault because others have never seen that side of the other person.

Money Cannot Buy Happiness

We were blessed to buy a beautiful home in an upscale neighborhood. It was a large, beautiful home of about 4,000 square feet with a large, gorgeous swimming pool and a beautiful, manicured yard with one hundred azaleas bushes that lined the front of the house and the driveway. The grass stayed beautiful because of the sprinkling system. It was an ideal home for what we needed for ministry. I entertained many well-known people that came to our church to minister, and I loved every minute of it. I had trained some of my most trusted ladies and we worked well together well when I entertained. Little did I know that some of them were waiting in line to be the next Pastor's wife.

I would spend many years later shopping my way to find peace. There was no store that could satisfy the longing inside me for unconditional love. The more I shopped, the more I wanted until it became a cycle that I could not control. Every time we had a disagreement and it was not solved, I would run off to a store. Not just any store, but the most expensive one I could drive to. I would come back home with my car loaded after spending sometimes thousands of dollars. Oh, I worked for every dollar at that church, even doing things he did not want me to do. All I ever wanted was for him to just love me.

Sometimes after he was making up after an argument he would go out and buy me something expensive, I would thank him but later I would lovingly say that he could save a lot of money if you would just be nice to me. He would laugh, but I was so serious each time. He seems like he never understood it was not the thing I wanted from him; I just loved him, and I wanted him to love me too. When we met, he had nothing, when I married him, he had nothing, only sixty-five dollars in his pocket. I spent my life trying to get him to do something that he could not do, and that was to love me like Christ, with unconditional love. He only knew how to give his way out of problems, which do not solve the situation.

So, I continued to spend until I was in debt. It was all temporary until the next blowout came. So, I tried to make myself happy, and just for a while, I was contented. Not very few women I knew could go into any high-end store and purchase some of the things I brought. When I look back now, I was just a dressed-up broken woman who needed to be loved.

Certain things still trigger my shopping sprees, like walking through the men's department. Recently, I was at a store and I parked on the wrong side, so I had to go through the men's department. Looking at all the men's things reminded me of all the money I spent on my husband. I always thought of him when I was shopping. Even if I were upset with him, I would sometimes buy him a gift to take with me home. I know what you must be thinking, but can I say; I really loved him even if we were not speaking to each other.

Where Do I Go From Here?

In 2009, my worst fears happened. My husband announces that after 40 years, he did not love me anymore and he wanted a divorce. We had just finished communion when he made the announcement. I was devastated! I suffered a breakdown and I had plans to take my life. One night, I was in my car and I had planned to use the effortless way out…Carbonize. I thought about my son so I wanted to say goodbye in a way that he would not know what I was doing. When he answered the phone the gift of discerning kicked in. He started to ask questions. He said, "Mom, where are you?" I tried to lie. Instead of lying, I told the truth, that I was in my car. I know what you are thinking. Oh, now you are worried about lying and you want to kill yourself. Okay, I know, that does not make any sense. But I thank God that Chuck saw clean through my plan. He said, "Mama, get out of the car and go into the house. Get on your knees and pray. When you get up, call me." Of course, I broke down in tears and did what the man of God said. Later, I had another episode at the mental health office. My granddaughter was listed as my emergency contact. The doctor called her, and she involuntarily had me committed. I made it through that crisis only because I made God a promise. I said, "God get me out of this hospital, and I will serve you with all that I have." I got out but I continued to go to therapy for about 2 years. The doctor put me on Valium and Prozac. One day, I heard, "Do not take anything. You must deal with this and embrace my will." I slowly stop taking the drugs, but my doctor thought I was still on my meds. Eventually, I was off completely, and God became my source of healing. I am not suggesting that everyone do this, but I needed to believe the report of the Lord! I had to have faith in God and trust Him that it would be all right. I was no longer working at the church, which meant I had no income. My husband made up lies to the people that I would try and take the church when he was out of the country. So, he had the board sign papers to have me ex-communicated. I could not believe that the few members that were left after his divorce announcement believe that I had that on my mind. The only thing that was on my mind was how I was going to survive, pay my bill, eat, and live. I was praying about where I would attend church. One day I was led to a church in Albemarle that I never dreamed I would be a part of or fit in with.

That church was called Albemarle First Assemble. The Senior Pastor at that time was Bob Gruver. He and the congregation made me feel at peace and at home the minute I walked into the parking lot grounds. I could feel the love and acceptance that I needed to heal. I would get up early and get dressed for their service, which was at 11:00 a.m. and I was back before my husband got out of their church around 1:00 p.m.... He just assumes that I was not attending church anywhere. I even overheard him talking to someone. He said, "She is not going to church." I never told him any different, I just laughed to myself. That was the best decision that I have ever made. That church became part of my healing and my family. When my son passed away, they came to my rescue in an amazing way. They helped with whatever I needed. To this day, I will never forget them that is why I still gives into their ministry to show my gratitude. There is another church that helped me in Badin, North Carolina. The Pastor is Frank Thompson at God's Church. Oh, I can say so much about these loving people. The pastor would allow me to preach to his people whenever he needed me. They, too were part of my healing process, and they showed me that God was not finished with me in ministry. Pastor Frank's sister, Ethel, would minister to me and bless me with fresh vegetables from her garden every time I was there. She invited me to all their functions, programs, and birthdays. I went because I needed to be around all the love that God's Church and First Assemble could give me. I went places with Albemarle First Assemble Ladies that I had never visited. I slept in the room with my pastor's wife, Char, who was the wife of Pastor Bob. She was such a wonderful woman of God. She knew just how to build me in the Lord. One day, I was at the altar, and she whispered in my ear and said, "You are beautiful inside and out." I just cried because that day I needed to hear those words. Do you want to hear what was so phenomenal about those churches? Their pastors and their congregations were both Caucasian.

My God Is an On-time God, Yes, He Is

Afterward, I did not know how I would make it financially. I was in the grocery store one day and I broke down at the meat counter. I cried out to God and said, "God no one is going to hire me, what am I going to do? He is sending a little money but not enough to pay the bill." That same day my spiritual daughter called and said, "Ma, God told me to hire you here at the group home." I almost lost it because I knew that God had heard me. I went to work for her, and she became my Ruth. Later, she said, "Ma, God told me that you needed to go back to college." My Ruth came to my house and took me to the college and signed me up to take the test. She would not take no for an answer. I did feel bad because I had not finished college. I fell in love and did not think about my dream anymore.

A Dream Came True

In 2010, I entered Stanly Community College at the age of sixty. It was always a dream of mine to go back. I felt bad because I had promised my Uncle Sim that I would go, which I did, but I got love-struck and did not finish.

I Went From The Pit To The Stage!!!

In 2013, I completed all my courses and I graduated with a 4.0 average with honors. I made the dean's list, and I was a member of the National Honor Society for Leadership. My Son, my daughter, my sister-law, and my spiritual children were so proud of me. But I was proud that I served a God who loved me enough to give me a second chance to do His will and to accomplish my dream.

My journey was nothing but a miracle all the way. The scriptures say, but my God shall supply all my needs according to His riches in glory by Christ Jesus. I went to school on grants and had money left over to pay some bills. I signed up to work outside of class in the food stamp department for school credit and received $200.00 for food because I had little income. When we say we are trusting God we should stop trying to make our own way. We need to walk by faith and not by our senses. God knows the end from the beginning and nothing I was going through was a surprise to Him. He had already met all my needs in the spiritual realm.

I was depending on my husband and the church to have integrity and help me. But instead, they tried to cover up the money he was still getting as if they could no longer pay him, which I found out was a lie. How did I find it out? It was through the leadership of the Holy Spirit. I remembered the bank passwords so I could track his account and his spending. I kept a bank statement that came to the house. My spirit said, "Keep it, you will need it." Oh, and I did.

The money was still coming, and he used it to do other things and support other people. He let the house go into foreclosure which meant I would be homeless if God did not intervene. But God gave me favor with the same realtor that sold us the house and our church. God put me in one of the nicest neighborhoods in the city. I always wanted to stay in Forest Hills. It was said to be for the rich or the wealthy.

Well, God wanted me to have the best. It was just what I desired. It was quiet and the neighbors were so good to me.

Now, for me to pay the rent on the house, I had to take my husband to court and sue him for alimony for all my faithful years. I thought about the 13 years I spent on Mt. Gilead helping and supporting him in ministry. I thought about the times I had to do without or wait because we did not have much money for extras. I thought about the few times that I sat at the table and had to pray that the food would come by faith. I thought about the times that I had to find a job to help us. He had worked as a teenager, which I never had to do, thank God. But it was with my help that we made it.

In my family, we always had plenty of food. Our lights were never cut off and we had more clothes than we could wear. He, on the other hand, said that they would sometimes have to wait until his father preached to eat because his father who was on faith had a bad heart and could not work a normal job.

I had never experienced a lack until I married him. When I married him, I had a diary to bring to the marriage. I had money in a trust fund that I would get when I turned twenty-one. So, baby I did not marry for money or to leave home. I was in a safe home. My mother was a real Christian who taught me through her life. Yes, I married for love! And yes, I still love the man I married but I had to face the truth that he is no longer the same man, and neither was I.

Please do not get me wrong, I was not perfect as I told you before. But I was faithful for 40 years, and that counted in the court for me. In North Carolina, a person can sue if they have been married for 10 years. I qualified for that. But every state is not the same. I am glad we never moved out of the country. God is not just good, He already knew what was going to happen to me, so He looked ahead and provided. That is why God has been my Jehovah-Jireh for years. Hallelujah!!!

No Weapons Formed Against Me Shall Prosper

In the months to come, I had to stand firm by a word I gave to my Church one Sunday morning. I did not fully understand what God was telling me but as I look back, He was not just talking to the congregation which He was, but it would prove to be for me as well. The Bible says that every story sounds true until someone comes and sets the record straight. One morning at about 3:00 a.m., I could not sleep so I log in to my computer which I did often to keep myself company. I would read Christian articles, listen to well-known preachers, and take notes on what I learned from them. I enjoyed learning about the word of God from other preachers. But this morning, I heard an unusual word from God. The word was "abuse". When I looked it up, I could not believe what I was reading. Some of the same things that I was going through were in the article. I like to help people, so I ran off copies of the article and passed it out at Church that Sunday morning. I never told anyone what I was going through at Church, not even my family. In some sick way, I was protecting his image and reputation, and my name as well. I was a pastor's wife, and I was ashamed of what we had become behind closed doors. Everything that look good had begun to unravel and I knew something was wrong that only God could fix.

He would say mean things to me, and he would just say to his congregation in his sermons, that when I got upset I would just cry. One day I came home, and I wanted some time with him. I mentioned how he had spent all morning with the men fellowshipping with them, so I want to do something with him. He seemed as though he just ignored my concerns. So, I must admit I was hurt, and I just walked away and went to my friend, my computer. In about a few minutes, he came to use our bedroom bathroom. This was strange because he passed two bathrooms just to use the one in the bedroom where my little office is set up. When he came out of the bathroom, I looked at him and as I turned away, he pulled out my chair that had wheels on it, and I fell to the floor. Then he pulled me up with my collar and pushed me toward the bed. It was so frightening that I reached for the phone to call the police. He then threatens to take away my job and income if I called. So, I called my spiritual daughter to drive me to my mother's house in Kittrell. I did not want to talk about what happened and did not tell my family. I cannot remember if he called his mother or if I did. I just remember that this was the weekend of our appreciation service that the church gave us every year and his mom told me that I should let him walk up the aisle by himself and I should not attend. Well, I should have listened to her, it would have been effective in his behavior toward me. That afternoon he came to Kittrell to bring me home. He came into the house with a perfume set and flowers. He found out that I was going to ask my daughter to come and bring me home to Albamarle, he was so upset with her. He thought or assumed that I had told her what happened. He went off on her and said some horrible things. It was devastating to her because she looks at him as a father figure.

I thought that things would get better, but they got worse to the point that I had to try to defend myself with a weapon because I was afraid for my life. He talked to his mother after he made the announcement to divorce me without any biblical reason and she convinced him to move out of the bedroom into the guest bedroom which he did. I felt like I was a prisoner in my home because I kept my door locked every night. I did not know this man; he was no longer the man I fell in love with and married. He had become a different person, so much so that he lowered his standards to the point of no return. He no longer cared that he was still married, and he did not care about his new life with other women.

Trusting God In A Crises

My husband finally moved out with the help of some of the members of his church. I could not bear to see him move so I left the house. I came back when he was gone. As I walked into the house, it felt like I was going to die. I could not believe this was happening. But reality began to set in when I walked into the empty rooms. I did not know at the time, but he was not supposed to move anything out of the house except for his clothes. We were supposed to go through mediation to settle everything. In North Carolina, if you have been married for 10 years can sue for alimony and everything must be divided 50-50. Those rooms of furniture should have never been moved until the court decided. Oh well, I did not know but God blessed me to get another bedroom set that was better than the one I lost. One day in 2011, I received court papers to appear in court for the divorce. I was so afraid, but I thank God for the support of my son, my spiritual granddaughter, and my spiritual daughter. Without my God and them, I could not have been able to manage. I did have a word from God through the scriptures. Later, I heard that my husband accused me of lying about not having money to give me every week. But I did not lie. He did not know that I got copies of his bank statements that proved to the court that the church had lied about the money he was getting from the members, and he was putting it in his account every week. After going through this painful ordeal, I won the case. I do not glorify in saying these things, but I need to tell the other side with all the integrity I stood on. One thing that I believe, you never have to compromise your integrity or your standards when you trust God with your life. Everything I said was the truth.

Holding On To The Words God Gave Me

I was praying one day, and I heard these words from God. He said, "I am going to bless you Barbara and I am going to cause men to give unto your bosom." And it happens just like God said it would. People had heard the news in the city. Some people just wanted to know the details, so I got invited to dinner a lot, but I did not give them what they wanted. It was amazing to me how God made all these people bless me without me asking or crying poor mouth. Every time someone saw me, I was smiling because God gave me a favor and they keep blessing me whenever I had a need. I was in the grocery store and a person walked over and said, I am going to pay for everything in you basket. There was another time when I only had 5 dollars in my pocket. The Pastor invited me to eat with her. Before she left the table she placed a piece of money in my hand. When she left I looked and it was a 100 dollars. I just broke down crying. It was mind-blowing at how many time this happen to me. I could write a small book on how many times it happen, I knew God was honoring His words to me. I am not saying that I did everything right because I know that I should shut my mouth many times, but I did not. I confess that I tried to change his character which caused a lot of hostility. I could not stand the way he treated the very people who loved him, yet he knew how to make their lives miserable when they did not do as he wanted them to do. One day he was so loving and without notice, it was like he turned on us. When I look back now, this started in my childhood. I hate to sound like the culture, but I hated the way my dad talked to my sweet mom when he could not get his way. My husband had been the same way. Yes, Mom and Dad spoiled me, and yes I am blunt but not mean deliberately to people. I saw him treat the preachers under him badly. They would do anything for him, but it always had to be his way or the highway, and he showed them that he meant it. It caused a lot of arguments between us, and I told him about it often, too often.

Forgiveness Releases A Harvest Of Blessings

Many years ago, I chose to forgive my father for the way he talked to my sweet Christian mother. I watched her forgive him and other people who felt she was too much of a Christian. They often pointed out to her how she should go to the streets like Daddy and party like he did. I love how my mother held her life to a high standard. Mom never wavered from her faith or her church. She was one of the most forgiving person I had ever witnessed. She was my example in many ways. She prayed a lot, and she choose her battles. I missed that lesson. In some way my husband was a hurt man even before he married me, and he hid it well. I remember the day I asked him to forgive me for my part in the divorce. I saw his car at the thrift shop, so I stopped. He immediately stood up from his desk and cursed me for being there. I ask my husband to forgive me for my part in the divorce." Then I left to teach a class on domestic violence, yes on domestic violence. I had gotten a part-time job working at a domestic violence shelter. I loved working there and helping other women face their crisis. It has amazed me how the article that I studied and passed out to my church for information that I ended up teaching the same thing that I experienced. I worked there for 6 years before I came home to Kittrell.

My psychiatrist asks me one day when I was in his office. Why did I want to be validated by a liar and a master manipulator? You may ask how my psychiatrist could say that about my husband. Well, it is because my husband called me crying one day after he left me. He sounded like he was going to hurt himself. I called the office of the place I was going to, and ask them to see him. At first, they said they could not, but I convinced them to please give him an appointment.

My husband went but said the same thing he did when we went for counseling. He told them how long he would go for counseling, and he did not go long. My husband really believed that nothing was ever wrong with what he did to anyone.

In 2014, our son passed away due to pneumonia and a blood clot in his lungs. He never called me to check on me. He never asked about the funeral arrangement for our son, and he would not walk in with me at the funeral service. I had to ask his nephew to be with me. To this day, I have not spoken to him since I walked over to him and gave him my condolences while the funeral was in session. He just bowed his head and never said a word to this day about it. I know now why I had to learn forgiveness. It would be a gift that I would need to give myself and teach others to do the same.

God Will Restore What The Enemy Has Stolen

I am blessed to know enough of God's word to believe that God would one day restore my character and ministry. My mother left me the house that I live in, so I did not need to go out looking for a home. My God is my Jehovah-Jireh, my provider. I was blessed to be asked by the Pastor of Kittrell First Baptist to teach the Bible study class for 2 years. Now, that was a challenge since I was from an apostolic ministry.

The things that I have been through do not define me, they only refined me. Joy does come in the morning and with it has come my passion for serving God's people. It has not been easy by no means, but God never promised that it would be easy. Someone asked me if I was ever mad at God. My answer was absolutely no. I know that I love God and that I had to keep the promise I made to Him while in crisis. I promised Him that I would not be angry. I needed Him more than I had before this crisis started. I am so thankful that I never stop depending on my God to bring me out of my mess. I knew it would not be easy because I did not know anyone who had gone before me who could help me. I knew it would not be quick, but some way God made me a promise that He would never leave me nor forsake me. I knew that God would not lie, so I had to believe God and ask Him to help my unbelief.

Today I am back home where I grew up. I never wanted to move back to this small town after living in the beautiful city of Albemarle. I was going through the process of healing after my son's death. I was not only surviving but thriving. Then one day, I heard God say, "Barbara, you need to go home. Your family needs you. I was not happy about that message. In April of 2017, I left my job at the Esther House Domestic Violence Shelter so I could prepare to leave Albemarle by June 17, 2017 which I was directed by the Holy Spirit.

At first, I was okay but the more I packed the more depressed I felt. I had been driving back to Kittrell to see my mother for 7 years after we placed her in a nursing home. I just could not see myself living in Kittrell. I had been blessed to experience a better life and I did not want to lose it. But because I love my God and I wanted to be in His divine will for my life, I obeyed Him and He has blessed me with more than enough. I serve a faithful God who loves me and does the best for me even when I do not see it in a natural way. You may ask if I still love Albemarle and the answer would always be yes.

But my passion to serve others has come with a lot of pain. Yet, it was good for me that I was afflicted because it drew me closer to God so I could learn more about His laws and about Him.

I can honestly say that God does restore what the enemy stole but I can also say that joy comes in the morning if you stay faithful to God. My God had a plan and a purpose for me to go through everything that he allowed. He knew that I would come out like Job in the Bible. When people ask me what college I went to aside from the two I mentioned… I told them that I graduated from the University of Faith, Persecution, and Experience (FPE University). And I am still working on my Ph.D. in Patience with human beings.

The Bible said that joy comes in the morning, but it never said which morning it would come. I just know that my God is faithful to do what He says. I just needed to trust Him with my life and believe that it was a purpose for my pain that was bigger than I could imagine. There have been numerous people who have been blessed by my walk of faith. Some I will never know about because they won't speak about it now, but they may speak about it at my funeral. Yes, it seems like I went to hell but the blessings that I gained were far better than the pain I suffered. My relationship with God is greater than my losses. You can always get more stuff but when you lose your relationship with God after having one, you are an empty vessel just making a lot of noise.

The story of forgiveness in the Bible is one that has helped me through the years. Joseph suffered for years at the hands of his brothers and others but in the end, he forgave them and took care of them. One day after their father died, they were afraid that Joseph wanted revenge. But Joseph said, what you meant for evil, God meant it for my good. I can say the same thing now to all my enemies. You meant to discredit me, but My God meant all for my good. In the words of David, it was good for me to be afflicted because it pushed me closer to God so that I may learn about his laws. I love the Lord more today because of what He has done and what he will be doing in my life. In all that I went through God never left me alone and he brought me through every crisis and I'm so grateful to him.

www.ingramcontent.com/pod-product-compliance
Lightning Source LLC
LaVergne TN
LVHW010413070526
838199LV00064B/5286